From Zumieta to Winnemucca

The Story of Grandma Fani and Grandpa Juan

Mayelen Garijo

Contents

GRANDMA FANI 3

ZUMIETA (GRANDMA FANI'S HOME) 7

EUGI'S FIESTAS 16

GRANDPA JUAN 19

PAMPLONA 21

FRANCE 23

GRANDMA'S TRIP TO FRANCE 26

HOME IN CALLE ARALAR, PAMPLONA 33

ARRIVAL IN THE USA 47

WINNEMUCCA, NEVADA 49

LIFE GOES ON 52

To my dad, Patxi,

and to all the Sunday excursions

that inevitably would end up around Eugi.

May the good memories last.

Adiós mi España querida,

mi vida queda contigo.

Y aunque yo no pueda verte,

piensa que nunca, jamás te olvido.

Author: Estefanía Egózcue (Grandma Fani)

Farewell my dear Spain,

my life remains with you.

And even if I can't see you,

rest assured you've never, ever been forgotten.

Translated by: Mayelen Garijo

From Zumieta to Winnemucca

My family has a story that has intrigued, inspired and enter-
tained us for generations. My siblings and the cousins I grew up
with in Spain spent countless hours talking about the family members that left, the ones that stayed, the ones that came back, and the
ones that we had never met. *Familying* was a pastime of ours. As
kids, we used to sit around naming and counting the aunts, uncles,
and cousins we had, admiring how handsome one was and how
beautiful another one seemed to us.

We would stare in particular at one picture, the one with Grandpa
standing like a peacock, tall and proud, behind Grandma who was
sitting on a chair. To her left, like a peacock's tail spreading wide
open, kid after kid, from shortest to tallest: Marisol, Alicia, Iñaki,
Juantxo, Anamari, Javier, Libe, Esperanza, Pedro and Patxi, all ten
of them. We only knew two of them, the two oldest, my dad Patxi,
and Tía Espe, my cousins' mom. The two of them had remained
in Spain after Grandma set off across the Atlantic with the rest to
meet Grandpa. We had no doubt when we looked at those pictures
that someday, we would meet them all.

Pamplona - 1952

All those family members we had not met yet were really not unfamiliar to us. We would hear our parents talk about Anamari and her very tall husband, Tom; Pedrito in the U.S. Army; Iñaki and Tía Marisol's husband's rock and roll band; Alicia and her beauty salon. We knew about their marriages and newborns. The news regarding the tíos and tías in America filled our thirst for family stories. We kids were over the moon when we heard that Grandma was coming back to visit. I was six years old when I met her for the very first time. My dad and aunt had not seen their mother for almost eight years. It would be twenty years till they would see their father. The anticipation of meeting either one of them was as high as this year's occurrence of the solar eclipse. We studied them and talked about them for years to come. Their visit gave us fuel for a few years, until the next set of tíos came over for a visit. Every time a new family member returned for a visit, we would fall in love with them.

The Garijo family story is the story of many, but it all started with these two...

Eugi 1932

GRANDMA FANI

A long time ago, almost thirty years now, while in Winnemucca, cousin Asun jotted down a few notes about things Grandma told her about her life. After finding those notes by chance, she organized them in a booklet and she gave us copies as a Christmas present in 2016. The notes were memories of Grandma's life, mainly about Zumieta.[1] Some things are a bit confusing, but Asun wrote them down just as Grandma told them to her. Asun also talked to Tía Alicia[2] from Zubiri and they added a few things.

Those of us who were lucky enough to have spent time with Grandma Fani and Grandpa Juan loved this gift and, right away, wanted to add a few of the stories we had heard as well. Besides, we thought it would be nice if everyone in the family could have access to the family story, regardless if they spoke English or Spanish. Therefore, we decided to add, as well as to translate, the stories we knew. It has been fun talking to cousins and uncles, and it has helped forge the bond of love that exists amongst the Garijo family.

Without further ado, we introduce you to:

---

1   Zumieta was the name of the house in the village of Eugi where Grandma Fani grew up with her family. In the late '70s, a dam was built in the town of Eugi to supply water to the residents of the nearby city of Pamplona. Zumieta was submerged into the dam's water.

2   Alicia from Zubiri is Grandma's niece who also grew up in Eugi, and moved to Zubiri after she got married. Zubiri is 7Km or 4.35 miles from Eugi.

ESTEFANIA EGÓZCUE SEMINARIO[3] was born in the village inn of Eugi, *La Posada*, March 30th, 1907. She was the fifth child of the nine children Francisco Egózcue Seminario (who, according to Grandma, had a really bad temper) and Mª Angela Seminario Belzarena had together. Their children, from oldest to youngest, were: Amalia, Sabina, Paco, Josefina, Estefanía (Grandma Fani), José (Uncle Charlie) and Felicidad, and two more who died shortly after being born.

Town of Eugi in the province of Navarra

---

3   Please refer to the Family Tree at the end of the book. Familyecho. com contains a more detailed file of Grandma Fani's extended family. If you want access to this file, contact me for log-in information. We can update the file as the family grows.

Photo taken in front of Zumieta:

Front Row, Left to Right: Francisco Egózcue (Grandma Fani's Dad), M. Angela Seminario (Grandma Fani's Mom), Pedro Garijo, Anamari Garijo (Smith), Javier Garijo
Second Row: Sabina Egózcue (Grandma Fani's sister), Amalia Egózcue (Grandma Fani's sister), Grandma Fani, Angelita Urrutia (Tía Sabina's daughter), Merche (Tía Amalia's daughter) and Grandpa Juan
Third Row: Tío José Mari (Grandma Fani's uncle), Javier Urrutia (Tia Sabina's son), Tío Períco Urrutia (Tía Sabina's husband), Alicia Urrutia (Tía Sabina's daughter)

uguko Zumieta ben la borda edo almazeneikin, karreteran
ra, ezker, Eskalapuin eta Beitikotxen bordak. Eskuin karre-
a berrie. Ximonéko andi borda dun: 11-IX-1970. E.L.L.

ZUMIETA (GRANDMA FANI'S HOME)

Grandma's family lived in Zumieta on the outskirts of the town called Eugi in the Basque Country. Grandma's uncle, Tío José Mari, who was a sheepherder, lived in the house with them, too. José Mari was Angela´s brother. He always spoke in Basque; his Spanish was extremely poor, according to Grandma Fani. Grandma grew up speaking both Basque and Spanish. When the second daughter, Sabina, married Períco, they too lived in Zumieta.

In the lower part of the house were the stables where they kept cows, a mule, sorrel mares, laying hens, rabbits and pigs. And of course, Tío José Mari´s sheep, which numbered over one hundred. They said that when he sold them, he was not able to sleep for five days.

Tío José Mari was single and had a limp ever since he fell from a window. He had a beautiful flute and played it very well. He would also sing along with his sister Angela, always in Basque, of course. They were very good singers. He sheared the sheep in the spring, then he would spin yarn on a spinning wheel, and that's how he would make *galtzamotzes,* which are very warm leggings that reach from the ankle to the knee. They would wear them even in the snow. Tía Alicia of Zubiri has vivid memories of him seated on the arm of the kitchen bench, *el escaño,* making the yarn.

The cows gave them milk that they sold at 1.25 pesetas per liter. They would obtain between 50 and 100 liters daily. The milk was sold in Pamplona and they had to have it on the bus that went to Pamplona, *la Montañesa,* early in the morning. Grandma Fani and her siblings would walk along with the mule that would carry the jugs all the way to the bus that left for Pamplona by 8:00 a.m. The mule, by the way, was blind.

In wintertime, they always killed two pigs and made blood sausages (*morcilla*), breakfast sausages, chorizo and ham. They put the pigs' thighs in salt to cure. At the remembrance of this Grandma exclaimed: "¡Qué cosa más rica!" or "What a delicious treat!"

Up front, at the right-hand side of the **borda,**[4] there were some stairs that took you to a very large door to get access to the living

4   In the Pyrenees, the term **borda** could be used in several ways. One, it is used to describe the home of a rancher or people who owned livestock. It was a home with two levels; the bottom one was used for the animals and the top one as the living quarters for the family and workers of the ranch. The term also applies to determine a geographical zone that would give the name to a mountainous area.

quarters. There was also another set of stairs that took you to the attic. The upper part of the door was always left ajar to air the space, as the kitchen was right in the front of the house.

CASA BALTASAR

Borda Prontxen

In the kitchen was a large wooden bench with cabinets underneath used to keep shoes. It was called *escaño*. This bench still exists. It is in the *borda de los mudos*.[5] It ended up there because some relatives of Grandma's, the Sazonas, bought that borda and they were given the bench. The kitchen also had a round table that would fold against the wall by lifting it, and a latch would hold it in place, just like the one they have in Zubiri still today.

The pantry was in front of the kitchen. They kept the food in big clay jugs. One of them was used to keep hard cheese, which they would use to make a paste that after fermenting was *Gaztamin*[6]; sometimes this cheese included worms. It was spicy and they would enjoy it with bread.

In another jug, they kept red bell peppers in vinegar. They used to eat these at *la merienda*, an afternoon snack. Other clay containers had pork loin fillets preserved in oil and lard, also chorizo and other meats.

La fresquera was a cabinet with a metal screen door that acted as the cooler and was left open at night.

To the left of the kitchen was Francisco and Angela´s (Grandma Fani´s parents) bedroom with two wooden, light-colored beds.

On the other side was Jose Mari´s bedroom, with one dark wooden bed and a trunk where he kept his flute, probably a txistu.[7]

Down the hall on the left was the bedroom where Grandma Fani slept with her sisters. Grandma Fani explained that in Eugi, kids started school at the age of 7 and they were done by the age of 14. "Imagine," she said, "seven years of school and of those I probably

---

5   **La borda de los mudos** is another house in the area of Eugi. It is common for all homes to have a name.

6   The famous **Gaztamin** is a cheese our parents, the Garijos, all remember eating in Eugi.

7   A **txistu** is a kind of fipple flute. This three-hole pipe can be played with one hand, leaving the other one free to play a percussion instrument.

missed half of them. One day we had to take care of the cows, another to harvest chestnuts, the next to cut ferns. We also had to go to the fields to take the workers their lunch."

Tía Sabina and Tío Perico had their bedroom on that side as well.

Opposite the kitchen, at the end of the hall, was the dining room with two more bedrooms on each side of it. One was Tía Feli´s room, which later became the room of Tío Perico and Sabina´s children. The other one was for Tía Severa; she was Tío Perico´s sister, who used to visit in the summers.

The mules were kept in the hayloft or **pajar** and the coal in the coal bunker or **carbonera**. They also had an oven where Tía Alicia of Zubiri, by the age of 15, used to make bread very early in the morning. All of this was located on the bottom floor of the *borda*. The grass clippings and branches had a special covered place, along with the machinery to cut the grass and turn it over.

In the center of the *borda* was a patio with a stone floor.

Aerial picture of Zumieta taken between Arancegi and Motxales.

In *la huerta,* or the garden, they grew potatoes, corn, lettuce, beans, carrots, cabbage, apple trees, plum and pear trees. One time, Tío Javier (Garijo) climbed a pear tree and Tía Angelita (one of Sabina´s daughters), in order to make him get down, told him the devil was coming, but Javier answered that he was going to scare him away.

The trough always had running water which came from the creek that ran down Mt. Gaztelu, a place where the family also had some grassland to feed the cows. The trough was also used to wash clothes.

Sometimes they hired help. Francisca from Urtasun[8] used to come to mend clothes. She would walk from Urtasun to Zumieta and was at the house by 8:00 a.m. sharp. Filomena from Mochales[9] came to do the laundry, *la colada.* First, they would soak the clothes. Next, they would scrub them. After that they would place the clothes in a bucket that was then covered with a large white rag. On top of the rag they would place some ashes that acted as bleach. They would then pour boiling water on top of the ashes. As they penetrated the rag, they would leave the clothes very white. They also had two servants living with them, Manuel from Sasuán[10] and another person from Urtasun.

They were hard workers and they worked many trades. For example, they would work with wood charcoal or *carbón vegetal.*[11] This was done mostly by Tía Amalia´s husband (Juan Pedro). First, they chopped up wood. Then, they would make a mound with it. The stack was then covered tightly with hay or bracken and dirt, to avoid letting air in. The stack would be lit and it would burn for

---

8   Urtasun, town near Eugi
9   Borda near Eugi
10   Sasuán, name of another one of the houses nearby
11   If wood is heated to high temperatures in a controlled environment with little air (oxygen) it will produce charcoal.

days. It had to be watched. Once the process was completed, the charcoal was placed in sacks and was taken to Pamplona to be sold.

This was done by either Grandma Fani's mom or dad, riding horseback, but they also did this trip on foot at times. When they had to spend the night in Pamplona, they would stay in "Casa Macaya," "Casa Baquedano" and also in "Casa Beltrán" in del Carmen Street. Selling all the charcoal was not that easy.

We also learned how they made cottage cheese using sheep's milk. They would heat stones in the fire and then they were placed in a container. When the milk was poured over the stones in the container, it would start a soft boil. A thick layer would rise to the top and it would be separated with a skimmer or slotted spoon. Then it would be placed on top of a wooden plank to drain. This is also how the cream was separated. It did not have a strong flavor.

The chestnuts roasted in the **tamboril**, a metal round cage, were simply delicious. They picked them with their spiny, very sharp burs in the morning, hitting the branches with sticks. They would make a fire on the ground and use a chain to hang the *tamboril* full of chestnuts over the fire.

They always made a cut into the chestnut first to prevent the nut from exploding. After removing them from *el tamboril*, they would place them on the ground and hit them with a mallet. They would drink sweet cider with these, always at nighttime.

They also grew corn, **el maíz.** After harvesting the corn, they would take it to the attic. At night, they would sit in low chairs to remove the husks from the cob first, and then any remaining silk until they were completely clean. The corn was then bundled and hung to dry. Next, they would rub two corn ears together to separate the kernels from the cob. The next step was to grind it. The animal feed was ground at home and the corn flour at the local mill. The old folks would complain that the miller always returned less than what had been delivered.

Once they had made the flour they would add warm water and salt. Then, they would knead it to make a thin round cake that was cooked over the embers of the fireplace, and they would eat them dipped in milk. They are the famous **talos**, that we have all heard our parents talk about.

Tío Javier described how they used to harvest **helechos,** or fern. *Helecho* was used because it was abundant and grew naturally. It was not cultivated. When dried, it was able to absorb moisture. Hence, it was used as bedding for the milk cows. It was harvested from the hillsides, usually in midsummer, at the height of its growth. This type of harvest was performed during a slow time on the farm.

The fern was cut with a scythe and left lying on the ground to dry. It was made into stacks, **metas**, at the location of the harvest. A tree about 6" in diameter was cut, the branches removed, and a point sharpened at the bottom. The pole was pounded into moist ground until it was stabilized. The *helecho* was stacked in a circle around the pole and tamped down by walking on it. More fern was pitched onto the top of the pile and tamped down until it reached almost to the top of the pole.

When the fern was needed, a platform was constructed with tree branches to transport the fern from the stacks to the road. The platform was hitched to a horse and dragged down the hillside to the road. Two or three *metas* may be transported in one day. At the road, it was piled on an oxcart and transported to the farmyard at Zumieta where it was used as needed.

After two or three weeks, the soiled fern would be cleaned out and stored in a pile for as long as a year. It was then spread on the fields as fertilizer.

Los carabineros, or border patrol guards, would go by Zumieta. They were shameless and they would spend all day inside the house instead of going to patrol the mountain crossings. They would sit by the fire while the family would freeze. They used to say: "patrolling at home."

Emigration was common in those days, and it was no stranger to Grandma's family. Grandma's brother, Paco, ventured in a boat to Buenos Aires. The trip was a month long and he spent Christmas at sea. He wrote home describing all the dishes they had served them for Christmas dinner. From Buenos Aires, Tío Paco moved to Montevideo, Uruguay, where he married a woman from Galicia. They had a daughter who fell ill and died at the age of 22. They said that after she passed away, Paco did not enjoy a day for the rest of his life. His wife worked for a German family. She never learned to read or write. Grandma Fani had written to her a couple of times and someone read the letters to her. Although she never met her in person, they had a picture they sent of Paco, Ascension, the wife, and their daughter.

EUGI'S FIESTAS

The townspeople used to have a great time, not only during the fiestas, but also every Sunday, because if the accordion player was around, they had a dance. Grandma Fani remembered how he used to close his eyes while he played. Tía Alicia remembers his name was Reveiro.

They used to dance slow dances, too. The person who liked to dance the most was Tía Amalia. Grandma Fani and Sabina also would dance, but Josefina never danced, and by the way, she became a nun later on.

They would have the dances in the plaza and in the inn. The drunkards would have to run home before dark, otherwise they would get booed.

During the annual fiestas, their house had two female servants and two male ones. The afternoon dances were folkloric ones accompanied by a *gaita,*[12] while the night dances were played with a guitar and a violin.

At *los piporropiles,*[13] they would eat cookies and hot chocolate in Loperena's house.[14]

Tío Períco bought the first washing machine ever seen in town. Grandma Fani said that the machine would prove to be great if it cleaned the clothes of the servant they had in Zumieta. The servant only had two sets of clothes that seemed to always be dirty. Tía Alicia remembers that the clothes came out very clean.

At around the age of 20, Grandma Fani went to Pamplona to learn sewing with Doña Seve Urrutia. There she met **Grandpa Juan,** who had a cousin learning to be a seamstress there as well.

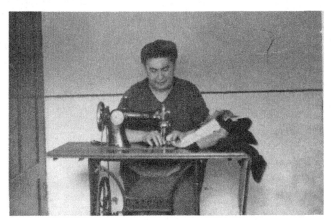

Tia Amalia (Grandma Fani's oldest sister) with her sewing machine.

---

12   A flute-like instrument
13   Dance parties where the girls would give the boys that danced with them a pastry
14   Loperena is the name of the house in Eugi where the family (Tía Sabina & Tío Períco, Javier and Nicolas) moved to in the late '70s when the dam was built and Zumieta disappeared under the water. This house was in the heart of town by the Plaza. In early 2000 the house was remodeled inside and converted into several apartments. Tío Nicolás still lives there.

When Grandma and Grandpa were dating, they used to take walks in the park of Media Luna, go to the theater (Teatro Gayarre), and to the street-dances in Plaza del Castillo in the summer evenings. Grandpa was working in Escurrida's woodshop at that time. This is where he learned his trade of "ebanista" or cabinetmaker. During Sanfermín they went to a bullfight, and Grandpa was dressed in the typical Pamplonican garb. They got married when Grandma was 24 years old.

Front Row, Lower Right Hand-Side Corner (Grandpa Juan wearing a raincoat and to his left Grandma Fani) at a bullfight during San Fermin, when they were dating (aprox. 1930 - 1931)

GRANDPA JUAN

Grandpa Juan was born in the Maternidad of Pamplona on July 11, 1908, at 11:30 p.m. This hospital also had an Orphanage Department. According to the records of this hospital, his biological mother, Isabel Eraso Ciordia, from Iguzquiza, Navarra, was admitted to this hospital on April 6, 1908. She gave birth to a boy three months later; the father was unknown. It was not uncommon for young unmarried women to stay at the hospital during their pregnancies. The following day, according to the records, Grandpa was baptized and given the name of Juan Garijo. It is unclear why he was given that last name, the record says:

...and the following day he was baptized in this institution's chapel, giving him the name of Juan and the last name of Garijo, the interested party is from Iguzquiza.

The document continues, stating that on August 7, 1908, he was given to Magdalena Vizcay, wife of Martin Villanueva, from the town of Olóndriz, Navarra, to be raised. Some documents show that his adoptive mom, Magdalena, gave birth to a baby on August 2, 1908. This baby died within two hours of birth due to pulmonary inflammation. After this event, she was examined by a doctor who certified that she was a good person, and her breast milk was in good condition for her to act as a wet nurse. There are no records of a legal adoption. We only have two documents, one from 1973 and the other from 1982, signed by the Ecclesiastic Directors of the Maternidad at the respective times, certifying Grandpa's date of birth. Another document shows that Magdalena Vizcay requested a baby for breastfeeding on August 7, 1908.

Grandpa never found out any information about his biological mother, not even her name. Not knowing who his biological mother was really bothered Grandpa. It was like an open wound for him. The adoptive family had four daughters and Grandpa always felt he was only wanted to work the land. He hated plowing the soil, and one day, he simply laid down the plow and walked away from the fields saying: "I will never work another day here."

One of the sisters was a wonderful cook, another one a seamstress. The oldest one, Presen, married one of her cousins and emigrated with him to Buenos Aires. The youngest one, Elena, left to become a nun, but before officially becoming one, she was rejected. She then emigrated to Buenos Aires where she became a nurse. When Presen's husband passed away, the sisters returned to Pamplona and moved in with the other two sisters that lived in Calle S. Ignacio where they worked as the caretakers of the building. One day, when Elena was on her way to visit one of the other sisters who had been hospitalized, she was killed by a car. Presen also became ill and was sent to a sanatorium outside of Pamplona, where she finally died. The other two sisters remained working as the doorwomen until they were too old and they moved to Casa de Misericordia, a home for old people in the heart of Pamplona. One of them lived there until she was over 100 years old. Tía Espe used to visit her there quite often.

PAMPLONA

When Juan and Fani first got married they lived with Grandpa's family who had moved to Pamplona, but shortly after they moved to **Navarrería street**, where they rented a room from a family with two children. This family lost one of the children during a bomb raid. Tía Espe was born then, in 1932. Their first three children were born in the Maternity Hospital, which was very close to their home, next to the Mercado, just around the corner in the same block. Grandma remembers walking to the hospital when it was time to give birth. Patxi, my dad, was child number two. He was born in 1934. Pedrito was number three. He was born in 1937. Later on, they moved to **la Calle Curia,** no. 12. While living here, the next-door neighbor punched a hole in the wall and the drywall fell into Tío Pete's crib. The neighbors were never fined or subjected to any kind of retribution.

Another anecdote during this time was remembered by Tío Patxi. Grandma had sent him to the grocery store to get bread; he was about three years old at the time. The grocery store, San Martín, was at the corner of Mercaderes Street and Calderería Street. All of a sudden, the alarm that announced the bombing raids sounded. A city policeman picked him up in his arms and carried him quickly to a bomb shelter near *las murallas*.[15] He wasn't sure how long they remained inside the shelter, but he remembered there were lots of

---

15   The stone walls that surrounded the city of Pamplona since centuries ago

people inside. Once they got out, the city policeman took him all the way to the doorway where they lived. Grandma was distraught and when she asked him what had happened, all he could say was that the man with the white candle had taken him to the Redín.[16] The explanation regarding the man with the candle was that the local police used to carry a long white baton in their tool belts.

Picture of "El Portal de Zumalacarregui," also known as The Door to France, in the park of "El Redín" in Pamplona. This is within walking distance of where the family lived.

In 1936 at the start of the Spanish Civil War, Grandpa was conscripted. He then decided to escape to France. Grandma left the apartment in Pamplona where they were living at the time, and with the three children, Esperanza, Patxi and Pedrito, went back to live in **Zumieta** with her family.

16   Name of the park where they still conserve the old stone walls

FRANCE

It is not clear when exactly Grandpa was placed into the refugee camp of Gurs in France. What is known is that he was arrested at his place of work, a farm. He did not have a permit to work in France. He spent about seven months incarcerated.

Gurs encampment was built by the French government between March and April of 1939 in the Atlantic Pyrenees area, 34 km from the Spanish border. Later on, after 1940 and during World War II, it would become a concentration camp where Germans held Jewish people of all nationalities. During that second period over 1,000 people died at the camp due to its harsh conditions, also succumbing to typhus and dysentery.

Gurs, a strange syllable,
like a sob
that cannot get out of the throat.
By Louis Aragon
Translated by Mayelen Garijo

Refugee camp that after 1940 became a concentration camp in Gurs, France

Initially, the purpose of this camp was to hold the influx of Spanish Basques that were coming into France through the nearby border because they were afraid of Franco's government repression. The camp was very rudimentary. The cabin-like buildings did not have windows or insulation and they were very cold. Since the area is close to the Atlantic, it rained a lot and water would get inside these cabins, which began to deteriorate fast, and outside it was often a muddy mess. There were no bathrooms and the residents slept on the floor in sacks filled with straw. There were no closets. The food served was scarce and terrible, and there was no running water. The camp was surrounded by double wire fences two meters high. These were not electrical fences. There were no watchtowers with police watching over them. This camp was different from the extermination camps of the Holocaust, or work camps, but the conditions were so terrible that about 1,000 men died there. The refugees were not forced to work and there were no executions during this first period of the camp. The camp was surrounded by other buildings that held the guards and the administration until October of 1940. After that the administration passed to the Vichy regime and it became a concentration camp. But the Spaniards, in that initial period, kept coming into France by the thousands, especially after the fall of Cataluña, and in the end, Gurs held a variety of people between 1939 and 1940. It had a capacity to hold 20,000 and at one point it held over 25,000. First, there were the Basques who had fought on the Republican side of the Spanish Civil War, against Franco. Of this group, practically all of them found local backing due to the proximity of their homeland to Gurs, and were offered jobs which permitted them to remain in France. As the number of refugees grew the camp also hosted a group of Republican Air Force men. Because this group had mechanical trades, many businessmen throughout France offered them jobs, which allowed them to leave the camp. Another group was composed of members of the international Brigades who had fought in the Spanish Civil War helping the Republican side, and who could not return to their countries. Finally, there were Spanish farmers with trades in low demand. No one in France was interested in them and therefore they were encouraged by the French government to leave the camp. The camp was closed in 1946, and simply forgotten until 1979. On the fortieth anniversary of its construction, young people in the area started to tell the story of the camp. They invited people who had been imprisoned there and gave conferences about what had happened there. Today, there is an annual commemoration, and the camp was reconstructed with a pavilion as a testament of the barracks that held the prisoners.

While in the camp, Grandpa had gotten news that Patxi was very, very sick. In fact, they had administered the last rites, thinking his end had come. Grandpa and another prisoner had been working on plans to escape. They were all but ready, when they heard that they were all going to be freed. The next day, everyone in the camp was freed. All the Spanish refugees were being returned to Spain. Most of them were *forced* to return to Spain.

Grandpa was afraid of returning to Spain, now under Franco's regime. While most of the refugees were taken through Irún, a town on the Spanish border, by train, Grandpa went back to working on the farm, until he got two letters attesting he had not fought against the regime. The fate of the refugees taken to the Spanish border was about to get worse. They were detained and sent to Miranda de Ebro camp. This was a concentration camp designed to "purify" according to the law of Political Responsibilities established by the new government of Franco. The prisoners there were used as a labor force. There were several camps like this one, all over Spain.

It was then that Grandpa sent word for Grandma to come with the kids so they could go to Venezuela.

GRANDMA'S TRIP TO FRANCE

Two years into the Spanish Civil War, Grandma got word from Grandpa. He was making plans to go to Venezuela, and wanted to know if the family wanted to go with him or if he should go alone. Grandma did not hesitate; she got the kids' and her clothes ready and decided to make the trip to France to meet him. They left Zumieta during the night, walking to Osaberri Mountain where Tío Jose Mari had a hut that he used when he was out in the pastures with the sheep. From there they continued to Urepel. They waited there until early dawn.

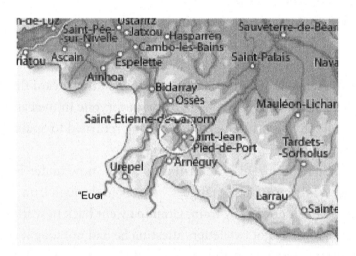

The map represents the border between Spain and France. The lower part in light grey is Spain. The Upper part in dark grey is France. Eugi is in Spain at the end of the line that runs above Urepel.

Tía Alicia from Zubiri still remembers how heartbroken she felt when she saw them leave.

Esperanza was about 7 years old, Patxi 5, and Pedrito 2. Although she was accompanied by Tío Perico, Sabina's husband, and Tío Pedro, Tía Amalia's husband, the group was directed by Juan Esteban, a smuggler who knew the area very well. Pedrito, the youngest at the time, would cry if anyone other than Grandma would pick him up, leaving Grandma no choice but to carry him all the way. They could not risk being heard by the border patrol and ruin their chances of meeting Grandpa. The trip was arduous, up the mountain, with the weight of a two-year-old in her arms. When they reached the French side, there were three men waiting for them. They took them all the way to where Grandpa was waiting for them.

Grandma Fani with Pedrito on her lap, Patxi in the background and
Esperanza in front
(This picture was taken around the time they made the trip to France).

They arrived in Baigorri, France, and they moved into a *borda* that had been abandoned and was in terrible condition. Grandpa Juan worked for a family in the nearby village of Azcarat, as a farmhand. They had a very nice neighbor who spoke Basque, and so Grandma had no problem with communication. In Baigorri they did not have running water and they had to travel with jugs to the river to obtain some. One day, Grandma was washing the clothes in the river and the current took the basket with most of their clothes. Tío Patxi remembered running down along the river to try and catch the load, to no avail. It was a great loss.

Ascarat, France

While living in Baigorri, Tía Libe was born. Grandma actually gave birth to Tía in Bidart, France. It was 1940. The story goes that there was a man that everyone called "Stavinski the swindler." He had a home that resembled a palace. Grandma did not know how he made his fortune. She thought he forged either art or papers. His house had an exit to the beach through the bottom floor. Grandma did not remember how that home was confiscated, but the government made it into a clinic, where Tía Libe was born. Grandma and Grandpa started walking to the clinic when she was in labor. On their way, a cart pulled by horses stopped and gave them a ride, with Grandma riding in the back of the cart. Grandma remembered riding the bus back home after Tía Libe was born.

(Bidart, France), town where Tía Libe was born. She was child #4.

Baigorri, the borda where they lived, was in the hills. Patxi was 5, and although little he had big responsibilities. Every morning before daylight, he would go get the milk jug and walk down the road from the *borda* to the neighbors' farm to get milk. He would run down holding the handle tight. On the return, his stride was slower as he could hardly carry the full jug of milk. He was afraid of the dark. He was startled by the wind, and some little animal crossing his path. He would trip and milk would spill from the jug. Once back home, he was yelled at because he had spilled too much milk.

They were waiting for the paperwork to be finalized so they could all go to Venezuela, when the Germans reached France. The borders were closed and the dreams of going to Venezuela disappeared. Grandma said that German soldiers would patrol the area, and a couple of times they stopped by the *borda* during the day, when she was alone with the kids. The soldiers demanded food and she would have to feed them what little she had, which left the family without anything to eat that day.

Grandpa had informed himself about what would happen to him if he were to return to Spain. He was told that if he could obtain two letters attesting to his clean criminal and political record, he would receive no punishment. However, if he was not able to provide the two endorsements, he would have to make up the same time in prison that he missed by not serving the military service. The letters had to be signed by high military personnel, a Commander of the Spanish Guardia Civil, a high-ranked church leader, a priest in charge of a parish or a city mayor. Once he obtained the two letters, the family started the trip back to Spain by train. At their arrival in the border town of Henday, France, right next to Irún, Spain, in front of Grandma and the kids, Grandpa was detained and taken away, even though he was carrying his two letters in hand. He was then sent to a concentration camp in Madrid. We have not been able to discover where exactly he was imprisoned in Madrid, as the details of this part of Spanish history were concealed for many years. Some have referred to these camps as *the forgotten history of Spain.*

What we know is that in these camps the prisoners were used for labor. According to Wikipedia:

"The prisoners were used as forced laborers -for reconstruction works, to mine coal, extract mercury, build highways and dams, and dig canals. Furthermore, thousands were used in the construction of the Carabanchel Prison in Madrid and the Valley of the Fallen-and the Arco de la Victoria. Later their work was subcontracted to private companies and land owners, who used them to improve their properties."

We do know that Grandpa Juan was asked to build the benches for the chapel of the prison he was held in.

Grandma, with the kids, returned again to Zumieta to live with her family. But first, she had to move to Pamplona where she lived with her mother-in-law, as she had to present herself at the police station every morning. They wanted to make sure that she was not going to leave the country. She then got help from Severa, the seamstress whom she had learned to sew with a few years earlier, and her husband. Severa´s husband was the bishop´s chauffer and talked to the bishop about Grandpa Juan and the family´s situation. After hearing about Grandma´s ordeal, being registered with the police station and having to present herself every morning there, the bishop contacted the police commander. Soon after that, Grandma did not have to continue her daily trips to the police station any longer. Needless to say, this is the kind of influence that the clergy had during the Franco regime in the country. Grandma Fani said that while her mother-in-law was always good to her, her sisters-in-law not so much.

Tía Libe also told us the story about when Grandma became pregnant with the twins. When Grandpa was in prison in Madrid he was allowed to make a one-time trip home. The nuns that ran the prison's chapel where he was being held helped him get a permit. However, his visit home had to be kept a secret. During his short visit in Zumieta to see the family, Grandma became pregnant. This was a conundrum, as people in town noticed Grandma became pregnant while her husband was imprisoned in Madrid. (There is a debate among some family members about this story not being possible.) What we know for sure is that the twins were born once Grandpa had been released from the concentration camp. They were children numbers five and six, born in the year 1944.

Giving birth to the twins, Anamari and Javier, was the hardest of all the births, Grandma stated. She remembered this was the only birth at which she had been administered anesthesia. It was a surprise that she delivered twins. No one was expecting this, not Grandma, and not the doctor. Anamari was born first, then Javier, who was much smaller, and the doctor said to Grandma that they didn't expect he would make it.

Grandpa Juan holding Anamari, Pedrito, Libe & Grandma Fani holding
Javier
The twins were born in December 1944

HOME IN CALLE ARALAR, PAMPLONA

When Grandpa returned from Madrid´s concentration camp
where he had been imprisoned, they all moved back to Pamplona
to Calle Aralar. They lived there for fifteen years and they hold lots
of memories of this home. The girls attended school at Sagrado
Corazón, an all-girls Catholic school run by nuns, and the boys at
Escolapios, also a Catholic school, just for boys and run by priests.

Later on came Juantxo. He was born in 1946.

Back Row: Patxi, Esperanza, Anamari, Grandpa Juan, Javier
Front Row: Juantxo, Grandma Fani, Libe and Pete

Next came Iñaki in 1949, then Alicia in 1950. Alicia was born on July 7, during the first day of the fiestas of San Fermín, and therefore no one knew she had been born. Most of the siblings found out a day later. And last, but not least, came Marisol in 1952. Grandma wanted Espe and Patxi to act as the godparents, but these two were still young, and too embarrassed to take that role. Instead, two friends of Patxi and Esperanza accepted to do the honors, Marisol Montaño and Jose Luis Razquin.

Grandma Fani, Alicia (baby, on Grandma's lap), Anamari, Javier, Grandpa Juan with Iñaki on his lap, and Juantxo in the front

Tía Alicia de Zubiri remembers that when Patxi got into trouble they would send him to Eugi as punishment. She also remembers that for a few weeks, Grandpa Juan was working in Zumieta making some furniture; when she and her siblings returned home from school he would stop them in the stairway and make them say: "*Bendito sea el Santísimo Sacramento del altar,*" "Blessed be the Holy Sacrament of the Altar," every single time they went up or down the stairs.

During the time that the kids spent in Zumieta, Tío Patxi remembered, the first radio was brought to Eugi.

This picture is not of the family, but it is representative of how entire families gathered around the radio in the evenings to listen to the news.

It was a Telefunken brand, bought in Pamplona in Casa Arilla. They could listen to two channels: Radio Andorra and Radio Independiente; the last one was against the regime. At the end of the Civil War the Nationalist forces, with Francisco Franco in power, issued a censorship order to all radio broadcasting, which meant that all news was obliged to connect twice daily with RNE, the National Radio, and re-transmit the government-approved news bulletins produced by the official radio channel. The Radio Independiente was a radio station established by the Communist Party of Spain in exile in Moscow. It was also known as *La Pirenaica* since there were rumors that it was broadcast from a location somewhere in the Pyrenees, which has been proven not to be the case. This station was in place from 1941-1977. Tío Patxi remembered best the songs that would be dedicated to different people. He also had memories of eating chestnuts, and the long afternoons when they were obligated to pray the rosary with his grandparents. Tía Espe remembers the fact that they dressed her cousin Angelita and her the same, as if they were twins.

During this time Grandpa had his own woodshop, and although he worked well, things did not always go right. One time, he had an order for the house of a high-ranked military officer. He built the bedroom furniture as well as a dining room set. He delivered it but did not collect the money then, and instead, they left town without ever paying him. Patxi and his friend Fermín remembered making the deliveries around Pamplona for Grandpa, not an easy task since they did not have a vehicle and had to push a cart with the bulky heavy furniture.

Above, building where Grandpa's woodshop used to be.
Below, just right around the corner from Grandpa's shop, their apartment building in Aralar 26.

This dining room piece was made by Grandpa Juan in the early 1950s. It now belongs to the daughter of Severa Urrutia.[17] It is in her house in Pamplona.

17   Severa Urrutia- She was Tio Períco's sister; she lived in Pamplona and taught Grandma Fani to sew. It was at her house that Grandma met Grandpa.

This dresser was also made by Grandpa Juan at the same time and it is owned by the same person. (Picture taken Feb. 2017)

The kids spent all of their free time playing in the street in the back of the building. They used to steal apples and plums from the neighboring *chalets,* the individual homes of well-to-do families in Pamplona. When they got hungry, they would go to the front of the building at street level and scream: "¡Mamaaaa la merienda!" Grandma Fani would come out to the window, and from the fourth floor she would throw them sandwiches wrapped in newspaper. Grandpa loved going to the movies, and that is what he used to do on Sundays.

Almost all of the siblings had their tonsils taken out. But Patxi had very frail health. During their time in Calle Aralar the doctors thought he had been infected with tuberculosis and were giving up on him. For the second time, he received the last rites. But Grandpa, not willing to give up, took him to a healer, who gave him some very tiny homeopathic pills, and Tío Patxi was feeling great within twenty-four hours. He lived to be 82 years old.

Tía Alicia from Zubiri remembers the coal shop that belonged to the Jauregui family in Calle Aralar, because she got her red coat really dirty there. Also, she remembers being almost electrocuted with a portable electric stove. She was struck by the electric voltage and could not move with the shock. Grandpa, who was in bed with a bad back, jumped out of bed like a lightning bolt to come to her aid when he heard her screaming in pain with great desperation.

Grandpa was unhappy with the Spanish government and wanted to emigrate to the US. A relative who worked at a textile business in Pamplona, Tejidos Erro, had another relative who had a ranch in the USA, and through him he got the paperwork to emigrate to California to work on a ranch. He left Pamplona in 1953. Marisol was not even a year old.

Back Row: Patxi, Esperanza, Pete
Front Row: Anamari, Grandma Fani, Marisol (in Grandma's lap), Alicia, Javier, Juantxo, Grandpa Juan, Iñaki (on Grandpa's lap) and Libe

Grandpa did not always send money; Grandma said: "I was left with all ten children." She said she survived thanks to her family in Eugi. Javier worked in a company that worked with rubber, and Patxi in a garage. She wrote to Grandpa, asking him to send her money, and he wrote back infuriated, asking what were all the lazy kids doing. Not long after that she got word from D. Jose Manuel, the local parish priest of San Francisco Javier, that Grandpa had written to him. She explained that he had left her with all the kids and was not sending any money, and that what the two boys made was not enough to even help themselves. The baker would not give her bread any more, she added. This went on until he fulfilled his six years in the USA, and was then permitted by the government to bring in his family. Grandpa asked her to go to an agency, Revestido Agency, to ask them to start preparing the paperwork necessary for Esperanza and Patxi (who were already 18 years old) to be able to enter the States with the rest of the family. She did as she was instructed by Grandpa, and the agency told her they would start the process. But, when the time came, the agency had other people who paid them well, and this family was given the permits instead. Patxi and Espe were not able to go. Grandpa was enraged when he heard about it. "In his letters, he was always scolding me," Grandma said. Grandma told us part of her life story, with a calmness in her voice, but she showed real frustration while talking about the episode regarding this agency. Her life had been very difficult in many instances, but it was only when she was telling us this incident, which she referred to as a *dirty trick*, that she could not contain her anger and sadness. Not being able to take the whole family with her really broke her heart.

While Grandpa was in America, Iñaki the eighth child got sick. It started with pain in his legs, and then he would fall down, unable to walk. A doctor in Pamplona had him under observation and he called a specialist in Madrid. They decided to admit him to a hospital in Madrid, a hospital where the son-in-law of Franco was a surgeon, el Marqués de Villaverde. It was a hospital for the rich. There Iñaki was diagnosed with polio. Since this hospital was very expensive and Grandma could not afford to pay, they were moved to a different hospital, all thanks to the doctor from Pamplona, whom Grandma was very grateful for. "In that new hospital, there was a nun who was worse than the devil himself," Grandma exclaimed. One day she told Grandma Fani: "Your son's treatment is going to financially ruin this hospital, it is 500.00 pesetas daily." Iñaki's surgery was done by a German doctor. They spent a month in Madrid. Tío Jose (Grandma´s brother) and Tía Puri, his wife, visited them in Madrid as they had just moved back from the Philippines. Jose had left for the Philippines at the age of 16. He eventually owned a factory where they manufactured rope. Grandma said she was able to survive thanks to her family. Tío José paid for everything during their stay in Madrid.

Alicia remembers very well when Iñaki returned from his Madrid surgery. She remembers how he would get all of Grandma's attention, as well as of everyone else who would come to the house to visit. Visitors brought him presents. He was always sitting in a chair in the kitchen, where Grandma could keep a close eye on him. One morning, Grandma had to leave to run some errands and left Alicia in charge of watching him. Alicia asked Iñaki to get up from the chair and walk. Iñaki replied that he could not walk. But Alicia insisted; she was a kid herself, maybe seven years old. She thought that if he tried he would be able to. All he had to do, she told him, was move one foot and then the other. She was determined to help him. He pushed himself off the chair aided by Alicia and, of course, he fell flat on the floor, his legs not able to follow him. She remembered the scene as if it were yesterday.

Pedrito followed in his father's footsteps and left for the USA three years after Grandpa, on his own, at the age of 18 or 19.

Espe started to work in an office and she would always say she could not do dishes because her hands had to look good for her job. Javier was 13 when he worked at the company Dumanu. Even though he was just a kid, they would send him to the bank to pick up the cash to pay the workers. He would ride his bike back and forth. He used to try to get close to the bus so he could grab onto a bar and be pulled up the hill on his bike. One time the police caught him doing this and they deflated his bike tires.

Tío Patxi had a girlfriend, the daughter of the owners of the grocery store. Many times Grandma had to ask for food on credit. Food was scarce. Alicia and Marisol remember Grandma telling them to stop at the grocery store before heading to school, to ask for a *galleta,* a small biscuit. That would be their breakfast. The owners of the grocery store were bringing coffee in contraband. The prices were lower and they avoided certain taxes. Apparently, they were trying to find a way to hide some of the coffee they had brought and they asked Patxi to see if he could hide it for a while. Patxi took the coffee bags and went to hide them in the attic at the building where they lived. The fourth floor had two apartments. Theirs was on the right. A single lady lived in the one on the left. The neighbor lady saw Patxi putting the coffee in the trapdoor on the ceiling at the landing of the stairs in between the two apartments, and she called the police on him. Needless to say, having for neighbors a woman and ten children was not to her liking. Patxi was arrested and taken to the police station. While in the police station he was interrogated and was made to hold a coin with his nose against the wall. When he let the coin fall to the floor he was hit and would have to start all over again. That was the end of the girlfriend, of receiving any food on credit, and any friendship between the owners and Grandma.

Tía Libe remembers money always being tight. One time, she was sent to the store to buy the bread and milk and she kept a peseta (the equivalent of a penny) from the change, hiding it inside her sock. When she gave the money back, Patxi told her that the change was not right and asked her where the rest of the money was. She continued to say that was all the money they had given her. But Patxi asked her to show what was in her pockets, then asked her to take her shoes off, and finally to take her socks off, where the small coin fell, rolling onto the kitchen floor.

They all attended English classes with a teacher in Pamplona. Libe and Espe would argue all the time, fighting about whose turn it was to do the cleaning, or the laundry, or polishing the shoes. Their arguments were constant.

As they grew up, Libe also worked in a store and was learning to become a hairdresser. They went to Eugi often. They took the bus, a trip of 17.4 miles that used to take them three hours. The bus driver and most of the men riding on the bus would get off in two places, Huarte and Zubiri, and would go to the bar to have a drink and chitchat.

Grandma almost lost a finger when she got a splinter and it got infected. A neighbor, who was a brute, wrapped it with some thin rope to burst it open. She finally went to the Red Cross, where they opened the wound and cured her. Another time, she was chasing Javier while she had "bayetas," cleaning cloths, under her feet to wipe the waxed floors and she fell down hard and burst her ear open. Afterwards Javier was going to receive a spanking on his butt as punishment. In anticipation, he placed a piece of wood under his pants, and Grandma almost broke her hand when she tried to spank him. At that time, Grandma's sister, Tía Feli, passed away. The doctor misdiagnosed her with pneumonia. Grandma's family called and said that they were bringing her to Pamplona. The doctor listened to her chest and sent her home. Grandma took care of her in Aralar, but she would not get better. The doctor finally sent her to the hospital and she got a new diagnosis, typhus. There she passed away. They were told that if she had been taken there early on, she would still be alive. Tía Feli was a teacher. She fell ill in her early thirties.

Espe started going out with Raul, even though she had another boyfriend at the time, whom they called "the black one." Grandma sometimes would be left at home by herself; one would be out with the boyfriend, the other would go to a local club that offered different activities like ping pong, movies and such for free, and the young ones would play in the street. But, Grandma had no free time to herself; she was always working. Patxi would ask her to make sure to iron his pants with one line, not two.

Patxi also remembered a time when at the age of 19, he took a trip with Uncle Charlie to Madrid. This trip was a reunion with five other friends that had been together in the Philippines and now they were all living in different parts of Spain. They stayed at Hotel Capitol in Madrid. When they arrived at the hotel Tío Charlie left, but first he gave Patxi a bunch of cash. Patxi was happy. He was left all alone in the hotel room, reading the newspaper, *el Marca*. The newspaper was announcing a game of *pelotaris*, and so he decided to go see them play at the fronton Recoletos. After some drinks, a taxi and the game, followed by a fun spree in town, Patxi returned to the hotel at 6:45 a.m. The concierge opened the door, saying: "Se le ha hecho un poco tarde," "Coming in a little late." When Patxi opened the door of the hotel room slowly, with fear in his heart and trying not to make any noise, he was surprised to find the room empty. Tío Charlie arrived at around 11:00 a.m., blind drunk.

While living in Aralar Street, something similar happened as when they were living in Curia Street. In the middle of the hallway wall, all of a sudden, a big hole appeared. This time there was no fine either. They nailed a wooden board to the wall to cover the hole, and that's all she wrote. Grandma didn't register a complaint as she was by herself and had no time for such a thing.

They did not have a washing machine at first; eventually they did get one, but it was not an automatic one. All the girls slept in one bedroom, and all the boys in another.

Grandpa Juan was not very pleased when he heard about his oldest daughter dating a *Pelotari*.[18] The two couples, Patxi & Angelines, and Esperanza & Raul, decided to get married. One evening after going to the movies, they went up to the house and announced their plans to Grandma.

April 29, 1959, a month before Grandma and the seven youngest would make the trip to the USA.
Raul, Esperanza, Angelines & Patxi

18   **Pelotari**: A professional player of Basque pelota, name for a variety of court sports played with a ball using one's hand, a <u>racket</u>, a wooden bat or a basket, against a wall (*frontis or <u>Fronton</u>*).

46

In order to pay the family expenses for the trip to America, they got a loan from a financier with the apartment as the guarantee. They owned the apartment outright. They had been able to buy this apartment thanks to an old real estate law by which, if the owner of the property wanted to sell the dwelling, and if the tenant wanted to buy it, the owner was obligated to sell it to the tenant and not to anyone else, and the sale price was in accordance to the rent being paid. This way they were able to afford the apartment in Aralar Street.

Brother and sister, Patxi and Espe, celebrated their marriages together on April 29, 1959 in the neighboring church of San Francisco Javier. The family left for the USA a month later, with great sadness. The family traveled to Madrid by taxi. Grandma Fani mourned over leaving Espe behind, living with her mother-in-law in what she referred to as a *shack*. Juantxo lived for that month before they left with Espe, Raul and Raul's mother in San Agustin Street. Patxi and Angelines at first lived in Aralar, but when they finalized the sale to pay the financier, they had to move out.

ARRIVAL IN THE USA

The trip was made by Grandma Fani and seven children, all except the three oldest. None of them could speak English. When they arrived in New York they had to show the X-rays that had been taken of Iñaki by a doctor that worked for the American Consulate in Bilbao. Raul had made the trip with Iñaki to get these X-rays. At their arrival at the airport they couldn't understand what was being said to them. There was a Cuban worker, but it was his day off. Another employee went to look for him and this Cuban worker was able to help them.

Marisol, the youngest one, had a hard time with the trip. Raul had bought a box of wine and a bottle of cognac to take as a present to Grandpa. In customs, they were told that they needed to pay five dollars. They could not put one cent together, much less five dollars. The Cuban worker lent them the money, and they gave him the bottle of cognac. Later on, they wired him the money.

In New York, they had to change airports to catch a second airplane that would take them to San Francisco. Grandma says that they were supposed to go to the other airport by helicopter, but because they held them at customs for a very long time the helicopter left without them, and they were taken to the other airport by taxi instead. They took two taxis and one of the taxi drivers was black. They had never seen a black person before. Juantxo, 13 years old at the time, was sitting in the back seat. Javier clearly remembers Juantxo licking two fingers and slightly touching the man's arm at the same time that he said out loud: "You should try and wash yourself once in a while." The driver just looked at him and laughed. Once they were inside the airplane Grandma was notified that they were a passenger short, and the missing passenger was one from her party. It turned out to be Juantxo, who had made himself comfortable at the end of the plane, seating himself in a window seat.

When they arrived in San Francisco, Grandpa was waiting for them. It had been six years since they had seen their dad. This was the first time Marisol would meet her father, since she was a baby when he had left. It was a bit of a shock for her, since she had always thought of Patxi as her dad. Grandpa took them to a diner in the airport and bought them all apple pie a la mode and a cup of hot chocolate. It was a treat that at the time, none of them appreciated. Every single one of them left it on their plate, although they did drink the hot chocolate. Tío Javier remembers that all the houses in San Francisco had TV antennas. They spent the night in a Basque hotel in San Francisco. The owner had a living room and turned on a color TV, and all the kids sat down without moving a finger, mesmerized by the TV. From San Francisco, they took the train to Lovelock where Grandpa had a car waiting for them. They rode all the way to Winnemucca, nine of them in one single car, arriving about 1:00 or 1:30 a.m. Grandpa took them to a hill and they could see the lights of the town. Tío Javier remembers that the boys were all in shorts and wool sweaters. They did not get much sleep that night. They were all up by 5:00 a.m. Javier was impacted by the big Nevada sky. It was a clear sky, it was warm, and he could not get over how much sky he could see.

WINNEMUCCA, NEVADA

Their first home was across from the Catholic church, a small house with no comforts. This home was temporary while Grandpa built a home of their own on Eisenhower Street; everybody chipped in with the building. Their new home had five bedrooms, a big kitchen and two bathrooms. After work, Grandma would help paint the new house inside and then she would fix dinner for all.

The very same week they arrived, Grandma had started work at the Humboldt Hotel (which burned down later on). She worked for a Basque lady who was not very kind to any of the employees.

Grandma worked in many places: at the Bull Head Motel with another Basque lady, Inda; at the laundromat; at the Holiday Inn Hotel; at the Winners Casino; at the Star Broiler; for the Mackie family as their housekeeper. She liked that last job. She could walk to their house.

On one of their first mornings in Winnemucca, Javier and Juantxo went out to explore the town. They found the local pool, and two boys their age shot them with a bean shooter, and took off running. Javier and Juantxo decided to followed them. The boys kept giving them the finger, and Javier and Juantxo could not understand what the deal was with their fingers. They ended up getting into a push-and-shove kind of fight. They also ran into a boy named Alfonso who was from Navarra as well, and he told them all about the finger and its meaning. The two boys became very good friends with Tío Javier and Tío Juantxo later on.

That first summer they spent their time at the public pool. When school started, Juantxo, Iñaki, Alicia and Marisol attended the grammar school. The twins and Libe went to the local high school. Pete had a job with some engineers, so he learned English quickly on the job. They grew up, and they started to get married.

Libe and Pat were the first ones to get married, next Anamari and Tom, then Javier and Robyn, Juantxo and Myrna. Libe was working at the Star Hotel and she started dating Pat, who was doing military service in Winnemucca, but he was from Michigan. Then the rest of the weddings came: Alicia, Marisol and Iñaki.

Pete worked as a sheepherder when he first arrived in the USA. Grandpa went to see how he was doing and the story goes that he found Tío Pete in the hills, with a pot of beans strapped to his back, herding the sheep. When Grandpa asked how much he was making, Grandpa did not like the answer. He went to visit the owner of the ranch and let him have it. The rancher told him to take him and his son out of there and never come back. Back in Winnemucca Pete lived with Grandpa and Jesus, Grandma's nephew who had also immigrated there. Pete and Grandpa could not get along, and Pete left for Idaho. There he worked at a Basque hotel.

Later on, he enlisted in the Army, from 1960 to 1963. For a while he was stationed in Germany and was able to visit Espe and Patxi in Spain. He met Tía Judy in January of 1964, they were engaged in April and married in October of 1964. They met in Winnemucca while Tía Judy was working as a lab technician at the hospital. She had graduated and had seen a job opening in Nevada. She decided to go on an adventure and give it a try. She rode the train all the way from Michigan to Nevada and was picked up at the train station by a police officer. Tía Libe worked in the hospital as well, and invited Judy to go bowling with her and a group of friends. Pete was one of the group, and the story goes that he liked her right away. "I especially liked the look of the back of her knees," he would say later.

The first one to return to Spain for a visit was Grandma, in 1967. Their visit was an awaited one for all of us living in Spain, but especially for Espe who had four children at the time, and Patxi who had three. Grandma's sisters and brother Charlie were very happy to see them, too. I, Mayelen, was six years old at the time and I remember the first time I saw my grandma. She was wearing black high heels and red lipstick, and she leaned to kiss me. I remember thinking she was the youngest-looking grandma I had ever seen. She brought presents for all the grandkids. The one I remember well was a perfumed stick of lilac scent, that worked just like a lipstick. You would turn the bottom and a bar would raise, and the bar smelled like lilacs. To this day, every time I smell lilacs, I think of my Grandma Fani. Her return trip was quite an ordeal. The airline personnel tasked with assisting her plane change in New York were negligent. Grandma knew the time the flight was departing and approached the airline agent. He had forgotten to assist her and was shocked when she touched his arm. She had missed the flight. There was no Grandma when the daughters met the plane. The Reno desk called New York, and Tía Anamari explained to Grandma that she would be on the next morning flight. However, she spent the night in a chair in the New York airport.

Grandpa did not return until 1973, twenty-one years after having left. Tom and Anamari went to Tío Pete's house in Michigan, where he had flown to meet up with them, to pick him up. The day before their trip to Spain they took a one-day trip to Canada in a motorhome. The next morning, they flew to Spain. Tía Anamari explained that Grandpa was amazed--one day he was in America, the next in Canada and the next in Spain. He could not get over that. He made a big deal out of it.

LIFE GOES ON

Grandma and Grandpa were successful in the States and lived a comfortable life. But, they had their share of problems with their relationship and ended up getting a divorce late in life, while they were in their mid to late sixties. Grandpa then lived at times in Guadalajara, Mexico, other times in Spain and the US. He never lost his adventurous spirit. During one of his stays in Spain, he lived with Patxi and Angelines and their three kids. It was during the seventies. All of us kids have great fun memories of Grandpa during this time. We were living on Aldapa Street, which happened to be right where the old maternity hospital had been, the one where Grandma had given birth to her first three children, and the very same place where Grandpa had been abandoned as a baby. The hospital had been torn down and an apartment building had been erected. We lived in that building on the fourth floor. I remember looking through the balcony down to the big hill that took you to the market, and Grandpa telling us the story of having been left in that very same street on the hill. He described the maternity entrance that had a big revolving door. When the door turned around, it had a bassinet attached to it, and that is where they would leave babies anonymously. Although I was young, I could feel his disappointment. He always talked about how he would give anything to have met his biological mother. It is strange to me now that he never wondered about his biological father. Anyway, at one point during the story, he stopped and said: "Son of a bitch, never better said." I remember my mother replying: "Aita, don't say that. You don't know her circumstances."

He had made-up names for all three of us. My sister, the responsible one, was *la patita* or "little mother duck," also at times *ganduna*, or "the oldest one." I was *chichita*, and many times *chichita patas de alambruno*, "little wire legs," and my brother, the youngest one was *chilito*. We learned to smoke and play some card games with Grandpa. My siblings and I were 14, 13 and 7 when he lived with us. He would ask us to light cigarettes for him, and of course we would fight to do so. "*Gandicaaaa enciendendunooooo*," he would call. My sister or I would run to the living room for the opportunity to light his cigarette, and take a couple of puffs. He also taught us to play the card games "Mus" and "Tute" and we would stay up late at night on weekends, playing cards and smoking cigarettes with him. One Saturday night, my mom got up complaining there was too much smoke, the kids should be in bed, and she was hoping he was not allowing us to smoke. There were three lighted cigarettes in the ashtray, and Grandpa said: "Oh, Sanabagun, I must've forgotten I had one lit up already." Cousin Iñaki remembers that when he first started playing cards with Grandpa, at the age of 7, they always played for money. Grandpa would put up both parts, his

53

and Iñaki´s. In time, Iñaki started to win. From there on, Grandpa didn´t want to play for money any more.

The game of Mus was one of Grandpa´s favorites. It is a Basque game that dates back to the mid-1700s. The game is played with a Spanish deck, which includes 40 cards. Playing Mus consists of betting on four different categories and trying to outplay the opponents by, at times, tricking them into believing your hand is better or worse than it really is. It is played in pairs and you use facial expressions to communicate with your partner. Both Tío Patxi and Tía Anamari developed a love for this game, and participated in tournaments in their community and beyond. Tío Patxi participated in the Spanish finals in the fifties. Tía Anamari, with her competitive spirit, and being the card shark she is in any game, played in tournaments with the Basque Club in Winnemucca. Her ability took her all the way to Bilbao for the International Tournament in 2009. No woman had ever reached that far into the tournament before.

Spanish Deck of Cards

I remember Grandpa being tall, handsome and always stylishly dressed. He used Old Spice. We all thought he was pretty funny. When friends came to the house they would be amazed by our grandpa. He loved to talk so much that we always were looking for excuses to get away from him. They saw him as somehow excitingly different. He had a funny accent, of someone who spoke Basque but with a mix of English. He would use English expressions in mid-conversation; two of his favorites were *sanabagun* and *anyway*. Every afternoon Grandpa would leave the apartment to go play cards with some friends or to take a stroll through town and then go sit at a park. Before he left the apartment, he had a song he would recite religiously. It went something like this, as he placed his hand on the different pockets where he had placed every one of the items:

Glasses,

Tobacco,

A lighter,

My wallet,

Moneta,

The keys

A handkerchief

And the beret!

Then, he would look at us and ask: "Did I forget anything?" Half of the time neither one of us kids would pay attention to him, yet were quick to reply: "Yes, Grandpa, you have it all." One time, he came back five minutes after having left. He was cross. He had left the house wearing his house slippers and we had not noticed. When he caught a cold he would tell us he knew exactly when he caught it: "I was making the turn for the corner, at the end of the street, when a cold wind hit me. It almost threw my hat off. I felt it. I got my cold right then and there."

Grandma always lived with one of her children after Grandpa left. She would take care of the grandchildren and continued doing chores until she physically could no longer move. I always remember her busy, with the laundry, the ironing or the cooking, and never complaining about any of it. Being around her family made her very happy. Grandma enjoyed making the local dishes of Spain. Here is one of her recipes that happens to be one of my favorite dishes:

BABY SQUID WITH POTATOES

Ingredients:
½ kg. baby squid (a little over a pound)
1.5 kg. potatoes, cut in cubes (place in a bowl covered with water until ready to use)
125 ml. olive oil
1 onion, diced
2 cloves of garlic, minced
2 small green bell peppers or Italian, diced
2 tomatoes, diced
Parsley
2 Tbs. paprika
Black pepper to taste
1 cup white wine

Directions:

1. Place olive oil in a pot and sauté onions and peppers until tender. Add garlic, and tomatoes.

2. Add Baby Squid and paprika. You can cut the baby squid in small pieces if desired.

3. Add white wine until evaporated, stirring frequently.

4. Cover with water and let it cook for about 30 minutes and the squid is tender.

5. Add potatoes and cook for about 15 minutes until cooked.

Serve with French bread and a green salad.

Grandma Fani developed arthritis and was bedridden for a few years. She would then lie in bed and watch tennis matches. She absolutely loved tennis. She was very well taken care of by all of her children. Any time you would visit her she would ask whoever was around to either serve you coffee or something to drink. She passed away at the age of 92, looking as beautiful as the life she had created for all of us.

Back Row: Iñaki, Javier, Patxi, Pete, Juantxo
Front Row: Marisol, Anamari, Esperanza, Libe, Alicia

At the beginning of this book, we described life in Eugi at the beginning of the twentieth century, while Grandma lived there. But it has come to my attention, through the cousins in Pamplona and some newspaper articles, that Eugi had a very rich history dating back to the eighteenth century. In 1766 the Royal Weaponry Factory was built inside the mountains of Quinto Real around Eugi. This factory employed hundreds of people, and its activity lasted until 1794 when the French troops destroyed it.

This factory was located in a very strategic place, since besides being next to the border with France, the area offered everything needed: wood to make coal, iron mines, and the water flow to move machinery. This facility mainly produced ammunition for cannons and light iron arms. The cannonballs were later used by the locals to heat milk and make *cuajada* or "curdled milk." They would find balls in the river and they would heat them directly in the fire. When they were hot they would place them in the milk to heat it rapidly.

The factory was acquired by Felipe II and lots of gunsmiths from Milan came to work there. Many different arms and equipment of war and defense were made there, as well as the children's armor for Felipe III and Felipe IV that have been preserved in the Madrid Arms Museum. They are considered among the best in the world.

If you noticed, both of Grandma's parents had the last name of Seminario. This last name came from one of the armor forgers from Milan, Juan Bautista Seminari. He liked the area so much that he stayed and married someone local. They had fourteen male children. We are descendants of one of their children. That is why the name Seminario is quite common in the town of Eugi.

While putting these stories together, some information regarding the prisoners of Gurs was made public. During a recent talk in September 2017, in the town of Pamplona, it was announced that a homage was going to be celebrated in Gurs, France, on Saturday, September 30, 2017 to honor the men and women of the province of Navarra that had been imprisoned there. Similar celebrations had taken place many years before for prisoners of other provinces. This came about almost eighty years after Grandpa Juan's imprisonment. An organization within the Government of Navarra, in the Department of Historical Memory, had invited relatives of those Navarros who had been imprisoned in Gurs to attend the homage in France. The initial talk was in Pamplona, and some of our family members attended the event in hopes of finding out specific information about Grandpa Juan. When was he there? For how long? Was there any data about his circumstances? Although none of our relatives were able to attend the homage in Gurs, at the Pamplona event they discovered that the Government of Navarra was planning on putting up a plaque with about 500 names of Navarros that had been imprisoned in Gurs. Lists of Spanish and Basque Gurs prisoners had been made available for public access. Grandpa's name did not figure in their lists. However, we had the chance to contact someone in the Department of Historical Memory: *Paz, Convivencia y Derechos Humanos* to inquire further. We discovered that the original lists of prisoners had been burnt in Pau, France, at the end of WWII. The current lists had been compiled by the Basque Government in exile. The Government of Navarra knew that their lists were not complete, and told us of many other families that had contacted them to point this out. We were also told that although we were too late to add Grandpa's name to the plaque, they would add Juan Garijo Esposito (Villanueva) to update their lists. I feel like it is a small triumph to recognize those who silently suffered under Franco's regime.

To learn more about this camp and see some images go to: https://www.facebook.com/RelacionesCiudadanasNA/videos/168538250365071/

ACKNOWLEDGEMENTS

Thank you so much to Asun Jimenez Garijo, who started the idea for this book many years ago. For making the first recording of Grandma in 1988, and for putting that long recorded conversation in a booklet format. This book would have never come to be without her exuberant and contagious love for the family.

Many thanks also to Tío Javier, who shared with me not only stories but also documents from Grandpa's past. Special thanks go to Tia Robyn who kept my prepositions honest, and my commas in check.

Some very special thanks also go to Tia Anamari for parting with her collection of pictures so I could make copies, and for her amazing memory with dates and such. To Tías Libe and Ali for sharing stories as well.

Also, to Kiko for putting in the time to look through old files of the Maternidad and discover the information regarding Grandpa Juan's birth mother. To my sister Josune for encouraging me to finish what I had started, because in her words, this book was a *jewel*.

Big love to the Garijo family, old and young, in the old country or in the new world. We are all here because of them, Grandma Fani and Grandpa Juan.

BIBLIOGRAPHY

https://es.wikipedia.org/wiki/Campo_de_gurs
Diario de Navarra, Eugi: DN 5-10-14

http://www.familyecho.com (Tool used for Family Tree)

http://lugaresconhistoria.com/los-campos-de-concentracion-del-franquismo Miranda de Duero Concentration Camp- Picture

http://static.panoramio.com/photos/large/88862138.jpg, Image of a Meta

https://pamplonaactual.com/wp-content/uploads/2015/09/portal-de-francia-e1441971201869.jpg, Image Portal de Francia, Pamplona

https://upload.wikimedia.org/wikipedia/commons/3/32/Logor_Gurs.jpg, Image of Gurs Camp, France

https://cdn.csuk-solutions.net/uploads/45/15114-europ-camping-1.jpg, Image of Ascarat, France

http://www.vacances-location.net/locations-vacances/map-ex-tract/pyrenees-atlantiques/ascarat.png, Image of Map: Pyrenees and Ascarat area

https://media-cdn.tripadvisor.com/media/photo-s/01/c7/7a/14/bidart.jpg, Image of Bidart, France

http://img.over-blog-kiwi.com/0/93/44/87/20161007/ob_5279d3_esclaves-du-franquisme.jpg, Image of prisoners in Miranda de Ebro Camp, Spain

http://ljubusaci.com/wp-content/uploads/2013/06/Esad_radio1.jpg, Image of Radio during World War II

https://cardcow.com/images/set334/card00747_fr.jpg, Image of Hotel Humboldt in Winnemucca, Nevada

Egozcue Seminario (Gran

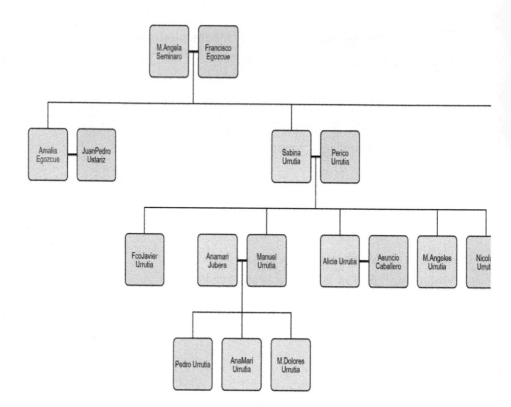

Grandma Fani's Siblings)

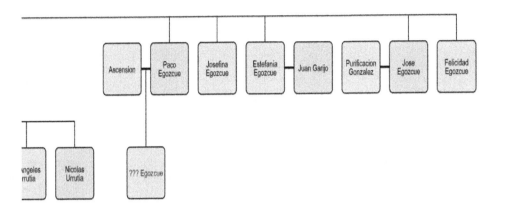

| Ascension | Paco Egozcue | Josefina Egozcue | Estefania Egozcue | Juan Garijo | Purificacion Gonzalez | Jose Egozcue | Felicidad Egozcue |

| ...ngeles ...rrutia | Nicolas Urrutia | ??? Egozcue |

Jimenez Garijo (E

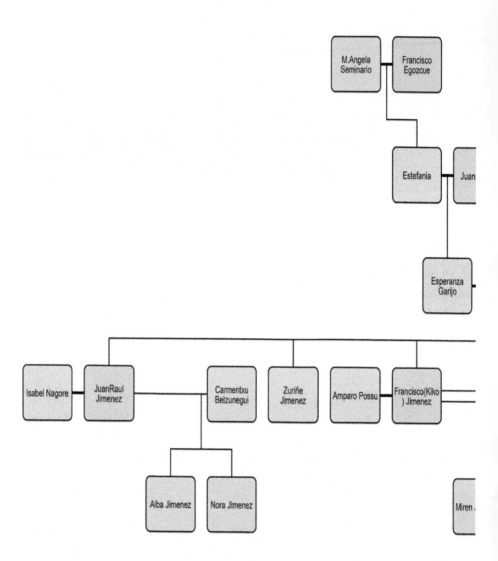

jo (Espe´s Family)

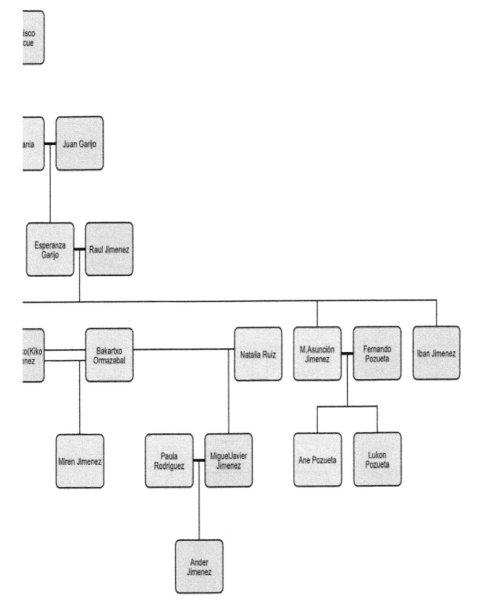

Garijo Erro (Patxi's Family)

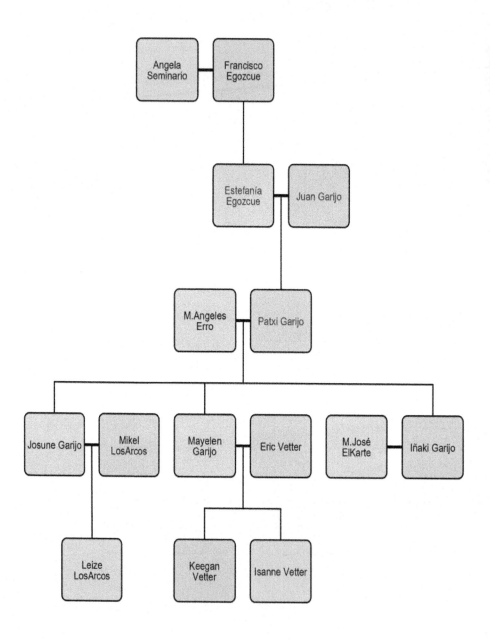

Libe McCauley (Garijo) Family

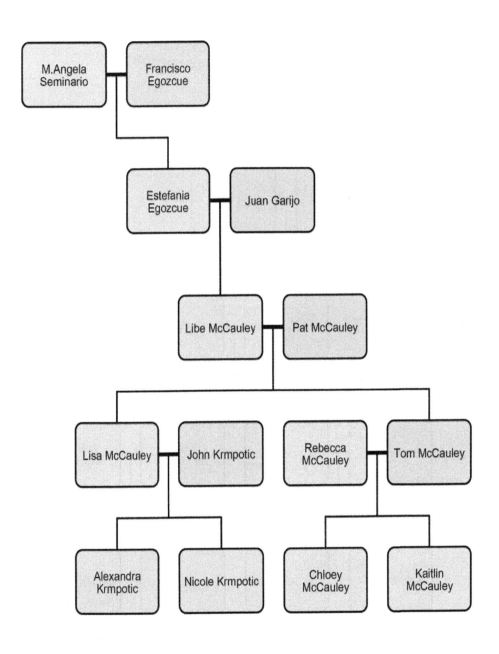

Anamari Smith (Garijo) Family

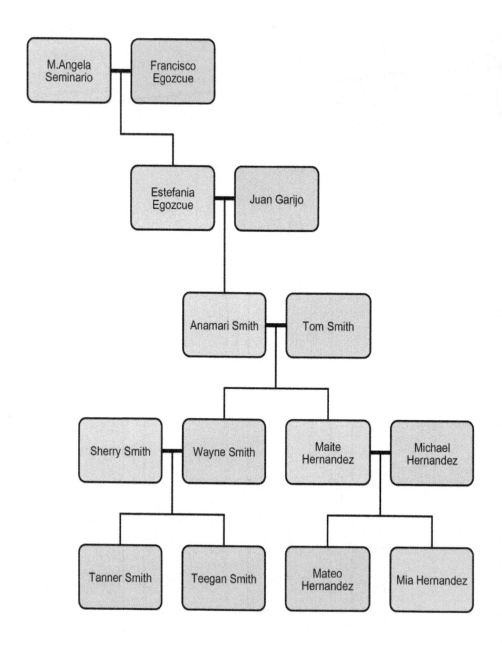

Javier Garijo's Family

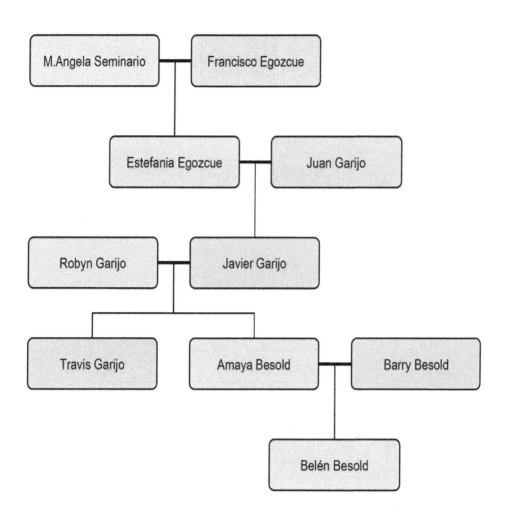

Juancho Garijo´s Family

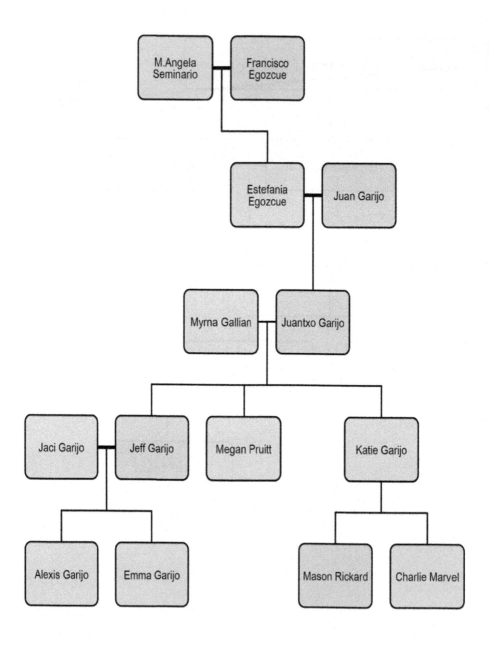

Iñaki Garijo´s Family

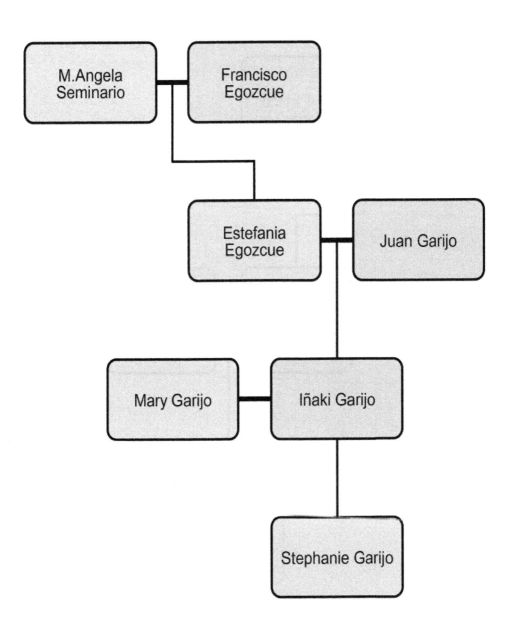

Alicia Garijo's Family

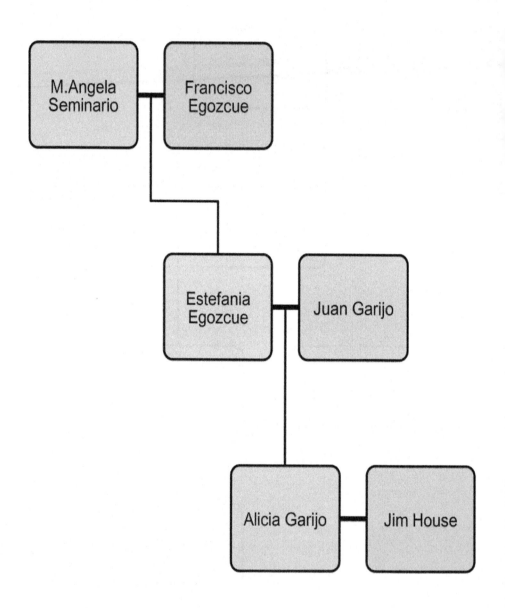

Marisol Bengochea (Garijo) Family

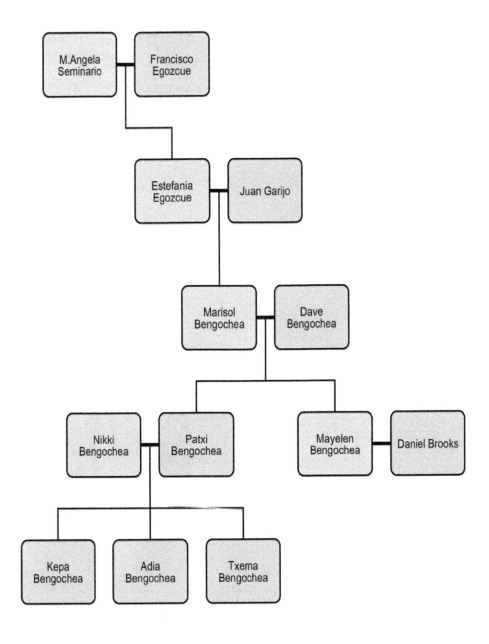

COMPLETADAS TRES CAMPAÑAS DE EXCAVACIÓN ARQUEOLÓGICA, AFLORAN YA EN EUGI DESTACADOS VESTIGIOS DE LA QUE FUERA REAL FÁBRICA DE MUNICIONES. UN EMPLAZAMIENTO HISTÓRICO DEL QUE CADA DÍA MÁS SE VE Y MÁS SE SABE, Y QUE CRECE COMO DESTINO TURÍSTICO. TEXTO Y FOTOS: **ASER VIDONDO**

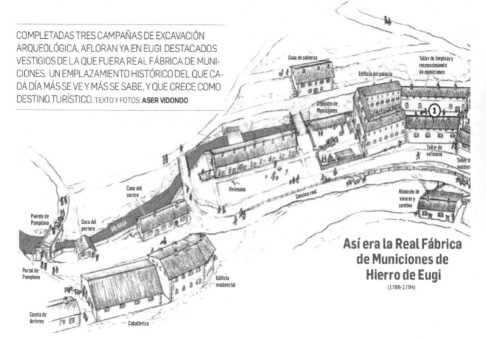

Así era la Real Fábrica de Municiones de Hierro de Eugi
(1766-1794)

Ilustración: Iñaki Diéguez Unibaso; Ana Carmen Sánchez y Paco Labé

Eugi rescata sus ar

EL 17 de octubre de 1794 todo acabó en llamas. El ataque fue inesperado. Se aguardaba que las tropas francesas pudieran llegar en cualquier momento cruzando la frontera, ubicada a apenas 9 km, y era lo que se vigilaba desde el fortín de la zona superior. Pero el enemigo apareció por la retaguardia, desde la zona de Baztan, provocando el desconcierto. Unos murieron. Otros consiguieron huir. Y el complejo recinto industrial en el que trabajaban, vivían y protegían hasta 500 personas fue incendiado y quedó prácticamente reducido a cenizas. De este modo se apagó la historia de la Real Fábrica de Municiones de Eugi, que echaba a andar apenas tres décadas antes, en 1766. Una historia, no obstante, que no murió del todo. Hoy resucita, está siendo desenterrada y, gracias al empeño local, puede ser de nuevo un firme puntal para Eugi, ahora como emplazamiento histórico de interés turístico.

Precisamente este martes culminaba en pleno puerto de Urkiaga, en un punto a 7,5 km al norte del pueblo, la tercera campaña de excavación arqueológica de la que se conoce más popularmente como "fábrica de armas" de Eugi. Tres veranos en los que la labor impulsada por el concejo de Eugi y encabezada por los arqueólogos Ana Carmen Sánchez y Paco Labé ha dado "unos frutos excelentes, algo que a la vista está". Así lo asegura la presidenta de este concejo del valle de Esteribar de 363 habitantes, Maite Errea. Y así puede constatarse sobre el terreno, pues las sucesivas excavaciones permiten comprobar una clara evolución año a año: muros de casi un metro que salen ya a la luz, el descubrimiento en una zona elevada de un fortín y un cuartel militar antaño ocultos, trazados del antiguo camino real empedrado que ya son visibles, paneles explicativos, nuevos accesos regulados para el turista...

Y la historia, que a veces es caprichosa, no lo es menos aquí. Precisamente quienes destruyeron en otro tiempo esta fábrica en el marco de la Guerra contra las tropas de la Convención (1793-1795), los franceses, son ahora socios del concejo de Eugi dentro del proyecto de colaboración transfronterizo 'Yelmo' con el que se recupera la memoria de esta fábrica. "Hemos trabajado codo con codo durante tres años con nuestros socios de Banca (departamento de Pirineos Atlánticos), donde existió un alto horno de bronce, y el balance no puede ser mejor", considera Errea.

Tal y como se aseguraba en su arranque oficial en 2012, si bien ya se trabajaba desde 2010, 'Yelmo' tenía por objeto mejorar y consolidar la relación transfronteriza entre Eugi y Banca a través de la puesta en valor del patrimonio minero-industrial de ambas localidades. Contaba con un presupuesto de 1,1 millones de euros, de los que 738.000 serían aportados por fondos europeos Feder que gestiona la Comunidad de Trabajo de los Pirineos.

Lo que se ve, y lo que no

En la parte navarra del proyecto 'Yelmo' se ha puesto en marcha el centro de referencia histórica Olondo, organizando jornadas culturales sobre

> Precisamente quienes destruyeron la fábrica de armas, los franceses, son ahora socios de Eugi para recuperar su memoria

> En los últimos tres años, además de excavaciones y estudios, se han realizado hasta 50 visitas guiadas para unas 1.800 personas

La excavación de este verano ha sacado a la luz casi un metro de muros en e
bases de muros de lo que fueron el taller de limpieza y reconocimiento de mu

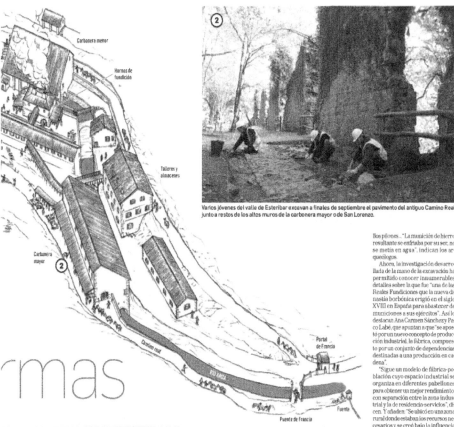

Carbonera menor

Hornos de fundición

Talleres y almacenes

Carbonera mayor

Camino real

RÍO ARGA

Portal de Francia

Fuente

Puente de Francia

Varios jóvenes del valle de Esteribar excavan a finales de septiembre el pavimento del antiguo Camino Real junto a restos de los altos muros de la carbonera mayor o de San Lorenzo.

rmas

l área industrial de la fábrica. En la imagen, dos personas caminan entre dos niciones (izda.) y el taller de refinería (dcha.).

las distintas ferrerías de la historia de Eugi (en otra anterior, también real y junto al pueblo, se hacían armaduras de lujo en los s. XVI y XVII para Felipe III y Felipe IV), configurado un paseo temático en torno a las armaduras junto al embalse, creado un sendero transfronterizo de unos 40 km o celebrado medio centenar de visitas guiadas para casi 1.800 personas. No obstante, el 'rey de la corona' ha sido la investigación y excavación de la Real Fábrica de Municiones.

El conjunto monumental comprende unos 10.000 m² de superficie boscosa del monte de Quinto Real. Atravesado completamente por la carretera N-138 en sentido Francia, hasta hace apenas unos años pasaba inadvertido, oculto por el arbolado y la maleza. Heredero de otras ferrerías que hubo en Eugi, aprovechaba los recursos naturales existentes en la zona: minas de hierro, madera de haya para hacer carbón vegetal con el que alimentar los hornos y un cauce de agua (río Arga) para mover de forma natural la maquinaria necesaria: fuelles, marti-

Jóvenes del valle sacan a la luz su pasado

Los tres últimos veranos, jóvenes del valle de Esteribar han protagonizado las campañas de excavación, contratados por el concejo de Eugi como auxiliares de excavación gracias a ayudas del Servicio Navarro de Empleo (Fondo Social Europeo). Este año han sido ocho y han excavado en la zona propiamente industrial y en el fortín, descubriendo muros y sacando algunos pavimentos como el de cantos rodados del antiguo Camino Real, junto a la carbonera mayor. También se han acondicionado escaleras, vallados y paneles de cara al turismo, y limpiado y documentado los puentes de Pamplona y Francia sobre el río Arga, ubicados en los extremos del recinto fabril. "Es una gozada poder colaborar en el descubrimiento de algo con tanto valor cultural", reconoce Urtzi Arrieta Puñal, de 24 años y de Zubiri. "Me sorprende todo lo que sale y lo que queda por excavar", añade su compañera Mari Munárriz Pastor, de 24 y de Eugi. Y Nikolas Gail Etxeberria, de Eugi y 20 años, sentencia: "Estamos encantados por ver cómo esto avanza, con lo que aprendemos y con que se apueste por dar trabajo a la juventud".

llos pilones... "La munición de hierro resultante se enfriaba por su ser, no se metía en agua", indican los arqueólogos.

Ahora, la investigación desarrollada de la mano de la excavación ha permitido conocer innumerables detalles sobre lo que fue "una de las Reales Fundiciones que la nueva dinastía borbónica erigió en el siglo XVIII en España para abastecer de municiones a sus ejércitos". Así lo destacan Ana Carmen Sánchez y Paco Labé, que apuntan a que "se apostó por un nuevo concepto de producción industrial, la fábrica, compuesto por un conjunto de dependencias destinadas a una producción en cadena".

"Sigue un modelo de fábrica-población cuyo espacio industrial se organiza en diferentes pabellones para obtener un mejor rendimiento, con separación entre la zona industrial y la de residencia-servicios", dicen. Y añaden: "Se ubicó en una zona rural donde estaban los recursos necesarios y se creó bajo la influencia del Enciclopedismo francés, con una moderna visión donde, además de la producción de municiones de hierro colado de forma autosuficiente y racional, cobraban protagonismo la salud y vida diaria de sus trabajadores".

Fruto de las investigaciones, se dispone ya, por ejemplo, de una reconstrucción aproximada de la fábrica a través de una ilustración que permite ver de forma gráfica parte de lo que constituyó este recinto, compuesto por lo menos de hasta una veintena de dependencias, atravesado por un Camino Real y con portales de acceso tanto en dirección a Eugi como a Francia. Esa ilustración, la que acompaña estas páginas, se puede repasar ya *in situ* en uno de los paneles instalados en el recinto.

"Esto fue algo grande. Tenemos un patrimonio de excepción y no dejaremos de sacarlo a la luz. Contamos con las *armas* necesarias para que Eugi suene fuerte como destino turístico", sentencia Maite Errea.

PASA A PÁGINA SIGUIENTE ➔

De Eugi, al mundo

Granada de 7,5 cm de diámetro hallada en Eugi.

LA REAL FÁBRICA DE MUNICIONES DE EUGI PRODU-
CÍA PROYECTILES DE HIERRO COLADO DE DIVERSOS
CALIBRES PARA EL SUMINISTRO DEL EJÉRCITO. SE
EMPLEARON SOBRE TODO EN LA ARMADA Y EN LAS
COLONIAS ESPAÑOLAS. TEXTO: **A.V.** FOTOGRAFÍA: **CEDIDA**

⊙ VIENE DE LA PÁGINA ANTERIOR

HASTA 1.000 tonela-
das de proyectiles
se llegaron a produ-
cir, respectivamen-
te, en 1779 y 1780 en
la Real Fábrica de Municiones de
Eugi. Un claro ejemplo de la im-
portancia que esta instalación tenía para la Corona española. Y su
creación en 1766 no fue banal.

"Los responsables militares de
la época, como el Conde de Aran-
da, vieron la necesidad de homo-
geneizar los procesos y calibres
ante los numerosos problemas
que daban las producciones reali-
zadas en fundiciones privadas: al
no coincidir los calibres, reventa-
ban los cañones si las bombas
que se recibían eran demasiado
grandes para salir despedidas, o
no se alcanzaba la velocidad de-
seada si eran demasiado pequeñas al perder efectividad los ga-
ses de expansión de la pólvora a
través del tubo del cañón".

Así, se fueron creando reales
fábricas de municiones "para te-
ner un abastecimiento estándar y
fiable", recalcan los arqueólogos
responsables de la excavación de
la de Eugi, Paco Labé y Ana Carmen Sánchez. Cabe recordar que
existen también en Navarra restos de otra Real Fábrica de Armas
y Municiones similar no muy leja-
na, en Orbaizeta (valle de
Aezkoa), junto a la Selva de Irati.
"Es de la misma época, copia el

modelo de la de Eugi en Quinto
Real, y es algo más grande", seña-
la Labé. Funcionó de 1784 a 1884.

Según los estudios que se han
realizado en torno a la de Eugi, se
producían allí proyectiles de hierro colado de diversos calibres
tanto macizos (balas) como huecos (bombas y granadas) para
emplearlos con cañones, morte-
ros y obuses. Algunas bombas lle-
gaban a medir 27 cm de diámetro
y a pesar hasta 69 kg.

"Los proyectiles huecos se re-
llenaban de pólvora prensada y se
prendían con una mecha necesa-
riamente más larga que la del cañón que los lanzaría. Por su parte,
las balas más pequeñas se solían
usar como metralla. Se metían
agrupadas en saquitos de tela y
hojalata, y se disparaban con el
cañón, saliendo dispersas como
los perdigones de un cartucho de
caza", destaca Labé.

Todo este suministro militar
iba destinado tanto a la Armada
(rama marítima del ejército) como a las plazas fortificadas en su
defensa de las posesiones hispa-
nas, africanas y americanas de la
Corona. "Así, desde el almacén de
la Real Fábrica de Municiones de
Eugi (Olaberri) se trasladaban las
municiones al centro de Olondo,
en el pueblo de Eugi. Posterior-
mente se enviaban a Pamplona,
donde estaba el centro logístico, y
viajaban hacia el sur y embarca-
ban en el río Ebro, siendo condu-
cidas hasta Tortosa (Tarragona).

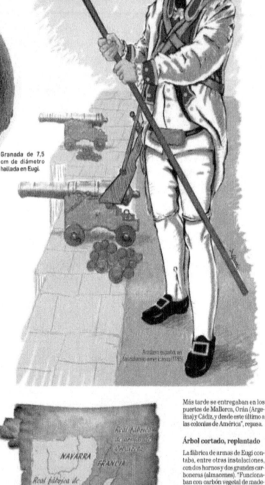

Artillero español en faccudismo-aime k:iros (1785)

Más tarde se entregaban en los
puertos de Mallorca, Orán (Arge-
lina) y Cádiz, y desde este último a
las colonias de América", repasa.

Árbol cortado, replantado

La fábrica de armas de Eugi contaba, entre otras instalaciones,
con dos hornos y dos grandes car-
boneras (almacenes). "Funciona-
ban con carbón vegetal de madera de haya y, con el objetivo de no
acabar con sus recursos, tenían la
política de árbol cortado, árbol
plantado. Contaban con viveros y
trasplantaban allá donde corta-
ban. Un dato: entre 1773 y 1789 se
plantaron 241.635, en su mayoría
hayas, robles y castaños. Un bos-
que de hayas se recupera en 50
años", apunta el arqueólogo Labé.

CPSIA information can be obtained
at www.ICGtesting.com
Printed in the USA
BVOW06s1731131217
502716BV00011B/73/P

9 781981 455539